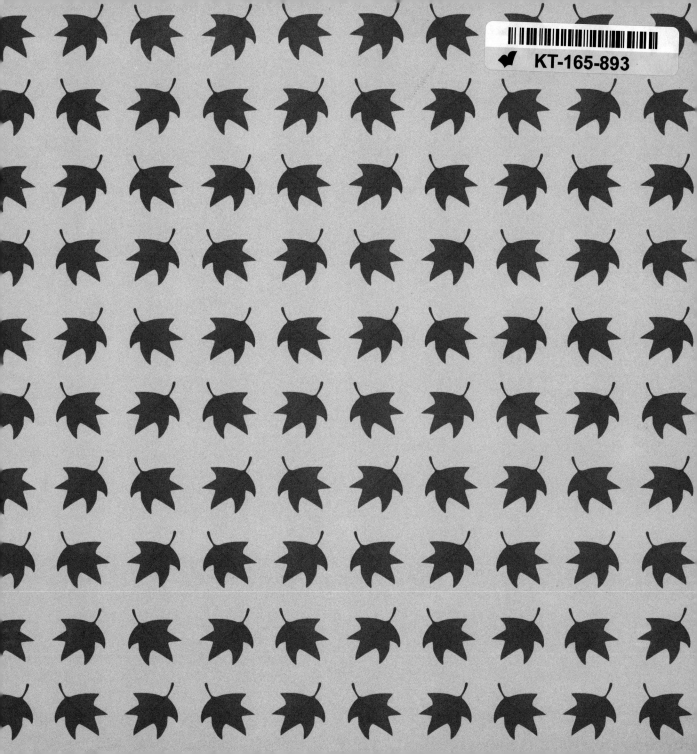

THE NEW LIFE LIBRARY

CRYSTALS

AND CRYSTAL HEALING

THE NEW LIFE LIBRARY

CRYSTALS
AND CRYSTAL HEALING

PLACEMENTS AND
TECHNIQUES FOR RESTORING
BALANCE AND HEALTH

SIMON LILLY

PHOTOGRAPHY BY
DON LAST

LORENZ BOOKS

This edition first published in 1998
by Lorenz Books

© Anness Publishing Limited 1998

Lorenz Books is an imprint of
Anness Publishing Limited
Hermes House
88–89 Blackfriars Road
London SE1 8HA

This edition distributed in Canada by Raincoast Books
8680 Cambie Street
Vancouver
British Columbia V6P 6M9

ISBN 1 85967 624 3

A CIP catalogue record for this book is available from the British Library

Publisher: Joanna Lorenz
Project Editor: Fiona Eaton
Designer: Allan Mole
Photographer: Don Last

Printed and bound in China

3 5 7 9 10 8 6 4

Acknowledgements
The author would like to thank the following people for the loan of crystals to photograph
in this book: Kay Harrison, Brian Parsons, Sue Lilly, Richard Howard of "Arcamia", Bath,
Mark O'Leary of "The Gem Mine", Exeter, and Mike Davies of "Evolution", Exeter.

CONTENTS

INTRODUCTION

Crystals and gemstones have always been highly prized for their beauty and for their healing and spiritual properties. Costly and difficult to acquire, gemstones have adorned the rich and powerful for thousands of years. Not only is this a display of wealth, it also expresses the hope that the qualities and virtues thought to reside in the stones themselves would "rub off" on their wearers. Healers, shamans, priests and spiritual seekers have continually been drawn to the clarity and purity of crystals and have made use of their special powers. Crystal healing as it is developing today

continues this widespread tradition by exploring new ways in which the mineral kingdom can help us restore balance to our frantic and stressful lives.

Science has yet to discover what is actually occurring during crystal healing, yet this in no way diminishes the real changes that are clearly felt by the participants and the lasting benefits that can be gained. Only by trying out a healing system for ourselves are we able to judge its worth. This book is designed to introduce you to safe and easy techniques so that you can see for yourself why gemstones and crystals continue to play an important role in our lives.

THE FORMATION, STRUCTURE AND PROPERTIES OF CRYSTALS

Crystals form only in the right circumstances. Deep within the earth's crust superheated gases and mineral-rich solutions at enormously high temperatures sometimes find their way along cracks and fissures towards the surface. As they cool, the constituent atoms, which until now have been randomly agitated, begin to arrange themselves into more stable relationships with their neighbours. This has the effect of building up regular three-dimensional repeating patterns of atoms, known as crystal lattices, in which every atom has found the most stable, balanced arrangement possible.

Crystals continue to grow until all the free atoms are arranged, or until the conditions change. As the solutions cool further and pressure drops, and as different elements join in combination, other sorts of crystals can appear. Usually, harder minerals – for example, diamond, emerald and quartz – will form at a higher temperature and pressure, while softer minerals such as calcite, turquoise and selenite crystallize at much lower temperatures.

A crystal may have remained the same for thousands or even millions of years, or it may have gone through several transformations of shape and form, dissolving and re-crystallizing, being subjected to new mineral solutions or new external conditions that have altered it in some way. (For example, the mineral rhodocrosite can metamorphose from calcite, which looks very different).

All the properties of crystals derive from their unique orderliness and the stability of their atomic structure.

Left and opposite: Crystals form in geometrical shapes according to their component atoms, the outer shape reflecting the inner structure. The cubic system forms crystals that are based on cubes, including fluorite, garnet, copper and iron pyrites.

So the energy and nature of a gemstone is a universal energy, one block in the foundation of life. Biological systems have evolved using the properties and characteristics of a huge range of minerals. When our own energy systems begin to break down under stress the simple, powerful resonance of a crystal may help us to clarify and reinstate our own harmonious patterns of health.

Whenever subjected to some outside force, such as heat, pressure, electricity or light, crystals are able to make minute adjustments that quickly restore their internal stability. This is the quality that makes crystals so important in many different areas of technology. We can find crystals used in watches and lasers, and as switching and regulating devices in engines powering everything from cars to space shuttles.

No one knows how crystals and gemstones can help the healing processes of the body. It may be that the very nature of crystals spontaneously increases the levels of harmony in their immediate environment. The introduction of a new element of order into a chaotic, disorganized state always tends to increase overall orderliness, because coherence is much the stronger force. Placing crystals, the most orderly matter in the universe, close to an energy imbalance, whether it is physical illness or emotional and mental upset, may encourage our own healing processes to become more effective.

The kingdom of minerals, crystals and rocks constitutes the physical matter of the whole universe.

Right: Quartz is one of the commonest minerals on earth and is central to many healing techniques.

THE CHAKRA SYSTEM

Knowledge of the chakra system comes from ancient Indian texts. These describe energy centres or chakras in the body, with seven major points arranged along the spinal column. These seven chakras are used in crystal healing.

Chakras are spinning vortices that focus certain frequencies of energy. When a chakra accumulates stress it becomes less able to assimilate and direct the appropriate energy into the body.

Each chakra has a particular focus of action but they are all interrelated. When one chakra becomes disturbed it can upset the functioning of other chakras. Over time this may contribute to physical illness or emotional upset. Depending on your surroundings and activities some chakras may be more active than others. It is best when healing to seek to achieve an overall balance in the chakra system, rather than focusing on only one or two areas.

Each of the chakras is linked with physical functions as well as emotional and mental states, and is also associated with a colour.

THE SEVEN CHAKRAS

- The first, or base, chakra is located at the base of the spine. It is usually linked with the colour red. Its main functions are physical survival, stability, energy distribution and practicality. The base chakra is linked to the adrenal glands.
- The second, sacral, chakra is situated in the lower abdomen below the navel. Its colour is orange and its functions are creativity, feelings, sexual drive, pleasure and exploration. It is related to the gonads.
- The third chakra is at the solar plexus, just below the ribcage. Its colour is yellow and it is associated with the pancreas and spleen. This chakra identifies and assists in the sense of identity, self-confidence and personal power.
- The fourth chakra is located at the centre of the chest and associated with the heart and thymus gland. Its colour is green and the heart chakra deals with relationships, personal development, direction and sharing.
- The fifth chakra is at the throat, by the thyroid glands. Its colour is blue and its concerns are with all kinds of communication, personal expression and the flow of information.
- The sixth chakra, often called the third eye, is in the centre of the brow. Its colour is indigo and it is linked to the pineal or pituitary glands. It is concerned with understanding, perception, knowledge and mental organization.
- The seventh chakra, the crown, is located just above the top of the head, linked to the pineal or pituitary glands. Its colour is violet and it maintains overall balance of the chakra system and channels universal life energy into the system. It maintains a sense of wholeness and stimulates fine levels of perception, intuition and inspiration.

THE SUBTLE BODIES

Crystals help to regulate the functions of the subtle bodies.

Much of the work of the chakras is concerned with maintaining a healthy balance between the different parts of the individual. The subtle bodies are the energy structures of each aspect of the self which interpenetrate, and extend beyond, the physical body. We are all aware of these non-physical areas of ourselves when we feel our "space" being encroached upon, or when we sense the mood of someone close by. The aura, or auric field, is a general term given to these complex interactions of energy, but they can be differentiated more clearly.

All subtle bodies maintain a flow of information and energy between them. When this flow is disrupted by a stress or trauma it acts like a shadow that blocks vitality to the system as a whole. Placing crystals within the auric field can work on these areas of stagnant energy, releasing them and realigning the whole subtle body system.

THE DIFFERENT BODIES REVEALED

• The etheric body is closest to the physical and provides the blueprint for the body and its organs. A disruption of harmony within the etheric body will almost always precede physical illness.

• The emotional body is the one we feel most clearly from others. It contains the ever-changing patterns of emotion and feelings. Being the least stable of the subtle structures it is the easiest to modify with crystals.

• The mental body contains the patterns in which we have organized our understanding of reality – our beliefs and thought structures – as well as our day-to-day concerns.

• Finer subtle bodies contain our spiritual goals and aspirations, our links to the collective unconscious, and the awareness of larger, universal energy patterns. These can be worked on with crystals, though it is less easy to define these subtle areas of life.

CHOOSING CRYSTALS

This book describes crystals and gemstones that should all be easy to find at reasonable cost. You can start with a very straightforward collection of stones, and the following guidelines suggest a basic working set.

• Small tumbled stones are very useful in crystal healing. For convenience, select stones that will not be too heavy when placed on the body but won't be so small as to get lost easily. Flatter stones will stay in place more easily than round ones. Aim to gather at least two stones of each spectrum colour (they don't have to be the same type of stone).

• Small natural crystals of clear quartz are invaluable. It is useful to have 10–12, each about 2–3cm /¾–1 ¼in in length.

• Small natural crystals of amethyst, smoky quartz and citrine are less common but well worth acquiring where possible.

• A small hand-sized crystal cluster of clear quartz or amethyst is useful for cleaning and charging your stones and crystal jewellery.

• Larger single stones and tumbled stones are useful to hold and to use as meditation tools. Work with one or two stones that attract you and that you feel happy with. It is better to work well with a few stones, than superficially with many.

Above: Whereas some crystals are hard, others scratch very easily. Even hard crystals may be brittle so store and handle them with care.

Left: Whether a crystal is perfect and clear or battered and grubby it will have the same internal orderliness and potential for healing.

CLEANSING YOUR CRYSTALS

New stones need to be cleansed before you use them. Cleansing crystals removes unwanted energy and restores them to their original clarity, so it should be carried out each time your crystals are used for healing. If you do not cleanse your stones they will become less effective and may pass on imbalances or energetic static. You might detect this as a feeling of heaviness or unpleasantness.

Right: Materials for cleansing crystals.

SUN AND WATER
Hold the stones under running water for a minute and then place in the sun to dry.

INCENSE OR SMUDGE STICK
Hold the crystal within the smoke of the incense or smudge stick. Herbs such as sage, cedar, sandalwood and frankincense are used for their purifying qualities.

Placing stones on a crystal cluster will clean them (left); alternatively surround the stone with clear quartz points (above left) for 24 hours.

SOUND
The vibrations of a pure sound can energetically clean a stone. A bell, gong or tuning fork can be used for this purpose.

VISUALIZATION
Take a deep breath and blow over the crystal. Imagine that you are clearing away negativities. Repeat.

SEA SALT
Use dry sea salt in a small container and bury the stone for 24 hours. Don't use salt water as this damages softer stones.

QUARTZ CRYSTALS

Depending on the conditions prevailing during its crystallization, quartz can take on many shapes and sizes. The different shapes can affect the nature of the crystal's energy.

DOUBLE-TERMINATED CRYSTALS have a point at each end. Most quartz grows from a rocky base and forms long, thin crystals with a single point, but if the quartz crystallizes in soft mud or clay it may be able to form points at both ends.

LASER WANDS are crystals that taper towards a very small, faceted point. Usually the sides of the crystal are slightly curved or bent. These stones are ideal for concentrating a tight beam of energy (hence the name), and clearing blocks and stagnant areas.

TABULAR CRYSTALS have two very large flattened faces, as though the crystal has been squashed. This shape increases the speed of energy flowing through it, so these crystals are excellent where extra communication is needed.

GEODES are formed where crystallization occurs in hollow rock chambers originally made by trapped bubbles of air.

HERKIMER DIAMONDS are small, extremely brilliant double-terminated quartz crystals. They are wonderful for energizing and cleansing the aura and are said to enhance dreaming and astral travel if placed under the pillow.

PHANTOM CRYSTALS are so named because within the body of the crystal can be seen smaller outlines of the crystal form. During formation another mineral has begun to crystallize on the surface of the quartz but hasn't inhibited further growth. These are fascinating and beautiful crystals to look at and they make good personal meditation crystals, exemplifying as they do the process of growth and "going within".

LASER WAND

DOUBLE-TERMINATED QUARTZ

HERKIMER DIAMONDS

TABULAR QUARTZ

GEODE

PHANTOM QUARTZ

DOUBLE-TERMINATED QUARTZ

SHAPED CRYSTALS

Ancient South American ruins have revealed stunning examples of carvings from huge quartz boulders. Today, quartz is carved and polished into many forms, some of which are purely decorative, while others can be of use in crystal healing.

Crystal eggs have always been popular – they are easy to hold and play with, they have stress-reducing comfort and they can also be used as a massage tool directly on the skin.

Crystal spheres have been used for centuries as a means of "scrying", or looking into the unknown, whether at future events or other dimensions. Large crystal balls are rare and expensive, but small spheres make excellent meditation tools.

Pyramids have a fascination for many and are said to have peculiar energy characteristics. They seem to create large powerful energy fields around them and can be useful for energizing a healing room or other large space.

The obelisk derives from Egyptian sacred architecture and is said to generate an energy field similar to the human aura. In a room, a crystal obelisk creates a powerful focus and balancing effect on the chakras and subtle bodies.

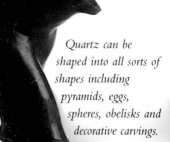

Quartz can be shaped into all sorts of shapes including pyramids, eggs, spheres, obelisks and decorative carvings.

THE QUARTZ FAMILY

Quartz is one of the commonest minerals to be found on the earth and has the greatest number of varieties. It is made up of silicon and oxygen atoms. Some varieties form large clear crystals while others tend to be made up of microscopic crystals packed tightly together in massive form.

Coloured varieties of quartz occur when a few atoms of another element are included within the lattice structure of the quartz molecules, distorting it slightly; or when another mineral crystallizes within the quartz as it grows. Because of their hardness and range of colour these stones are some of those most commonly found in jewellery and crystal healing collections.

CLEAR QUARTZ is colourless, water-clear and shiny. It may contain cloudy, milky sections or veils that are formed by small bubbles of water or gas trapped within the crystal. Rainbows are created by fractures or complex intergrowths of crystal that greatly enliven the crystal's energy.

SMOKY QUARTZ

CLEAR QUARTZ

TOURMALINE QUARTZ

AVENTURINE

MILKY QUARTZ

CITRINE

ROSE QUARTZ

RUTILATED QUARTZ

AMETHYST

AMETHYST is purple or violet in colour. Chevron amethyst has bands of purple and white. It is an excellent general healing stone which calms the mind and is good for meditation.

ROSE QUARTZ is pink and translucent. It rarely forms large crystals. Its energy is gentle but strong and it is a useful balancer of the heart centre and of the emotions.

CITRINE QUARTZ is golden-yellow or orange-brown. It occurs naturally or is made artificially by heating amethyst. Citrine is an energizing stone, physically and mentally.

SMOKY QUARTZ can be pale grey-brown to brownish-black. It is an excellent grounding stone and acts as a deep cleanser.

MILKY QUARTZ is white and contains a high proportion of gas or water bubbles. Its energy is softer and gentler than that of clear quartz.

RUTILATED QUARTZ contains crystals of rutile, looking like golden or yellow strands of hair or sometimes blades of grass. This variety is an excellent healer of torn or broken tissues.

TOURMALINE QUARTZ has embedded within it crystals of tourmaline – usually fine, black needles, but occasionally other colours too. This combination makes it an excellent protecting and strengthening stone.

AVENTURINE is a massive variety of quartz. Usually green but sometimes blue, it can be identified by tiny spangles of shiny silver mica or golden pyrites throughout. Green aventurine is a good heart chakra balancer.

CARNELIAN is a common orange to orange-red translucent quartz that is gently energizing and a useful healing stone.

CHRYSOPRASE forms in bright apple-green masses, a variety of quartz known as chalcedony. It is a relaxation stone.

BLOODSTONE, also called heliotrope, is a dark, shiny green with flecks or patches of bright red jasper. It is gently healing and energizing to the physical body.

JASPER is an opaque quartz of various colours. Most commonly it is brick red, but also yellow, green and blue. It is an all-round protecting and grounding stone.

AGATE is quartz laid down in different parallel, coloured bands, usually wavy or concentric. It comes in all colours though it is sometimes dyed to intensify the colours, especially in decorative slices of stone.

MOSS AGATE, picture agate, tree agate, snakeskin agate and many other types are all named from their colour or from the appearance of inclusions.

JASPER

OPAL

CARNELIAN

ONYX

CHRYSOPRASE

BLOODSTONE

TIGER'S EYE

BANDED AGATE

MOSS AGATE

BLUE LACE AGATE

BLUE LACE AGATE is another variety of agate, named for its delicate blue and white striations.

ONYX is similar to agate but has straight lines of white and black. (Sardonyx has additional brown layers as well.)

TIGER'S EYE is formed where quartz replaces an asbestos mineral to form characteristic plays of light across the fibres of brown, yellow, blue and red. It has an energy that is practical, stable and stimulating.

OPAL is a white crystal which forms in microscopic globules with a high water content, creating a wonderful play of colour. Opal is a stone for working with the emotions.

CRYSTAL HEALING TECHNIQUES: EXPLORING YOUR CRYSTALS

When you acquire a new crystal it is a good idea to spend some time exploring it. This is useful in developing your sensitivity to the subtle energy field.

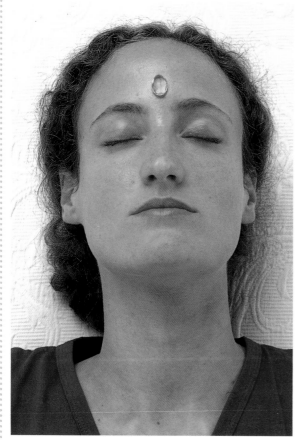

ABOVE: *Placing a stone at a chakra point will help you to identify what effects it might have.*

1 Look closely at your crystal from as many different angles as possible, then close your eyes and hold it in both hands for a minute or two. Note any impressions or thoughts you may have.

2 Hold the crystal near your solar plexus and, as you breathe out, imagine the breath passing over the end of the stone. Then, on the inbreath, imagine your breath entering through the crystal, directly into the abdomen. Continue this cycle to build up a circuit of energy, then relax.

3 Sit quietly with your eyes closed, then open your eyes and look at the crystal in front of you. Close your eyes after a few minutes and then pick up the crystal. Notice any changes in the way you feel.

4 Hold the stone in your left hand, then put it down and pick it up with your right hand. Repeat several times.

5 Place the crystal on your chakra centres – the most sensitive are usually the solar plexus, heart and brow.

6 Place the crystal close to your body while you are lying down. How does it feel on different sides of the body? Near your head? Near your feet?

A VISUALIZATION EXERCISE TO EXPLORE A CRYSTAL

For this visualization exercise, choose one of your favourite crystals, one you already know quite well.

1 Sit in a relaxed comfortable position, holding the stone in both hands. Take a few moments just to relax and focus on the crystal in your hands.

2 Slowly let your awareness float down into the crystal until you reach a point where you seem to come to rest.

3 In your mind's eye, identify how the crystal feels to you. Is it warm or damp, cool or dry, smooth or rough? Take a minute or two to explore the energy of the crystal through your inner touch.

4 Now relax again and turn your attention to any quality of sound within the crystal, whether it appears to be a tone, a pulse or a tune. Is it high or low? Simple or complex? Listen to the sounds of the crystal for a few moments, then relax again.

5 Take a few deep breaths, then imagine you are breathing in the crystal's energy through your nostrils. What smell, what taste does the crystal have? Can you identify it?

6 Relax once more, then open your inner eyes. Imagine what the structure and the energy of your crystal looks like: the quality of light, the images, the landscapes, scenes and figures that may be related to you. Don't attempt to analyse what you see. Just let the imagery play before your eyes.

7 Now become aware once more of the crystal's taste, its smell, its sounds and its touch. Very gradually bring your awareness out of the crystal and become more aware of your body and the world around you. Take notes so that you remember your experiences.

Right: Hold the crystal near your solar plexus and imagine that your breath is entering your body through the stone.

MEDITATING WITH CRYSTALS

Clear quartz has long been used as an aid to meditation and contemplation. Gazing at the water-clear crystal has a very quietening effect on the mind – you are looking into and through solid matter that has extraordinary order and stability. Contemplation of a crystal can help with problem-solving. If you have a

particular problem or worry, take a minute or two thinking about the situation and then gaze deeply into the crystal. Don't concern yourself with thoughts: just allow them to come and go. As your mind quietens down you may find a solution, or a new idea may pop into your head later in the day.

◄ Sitting quietly with your crystals will give you greater insight into how they work and how you might use them as healing tools, as well as developing your sensitivity to the energies. Sit comfortably and gaze into a crystal. Take time to look closely at it in detail, then allow your focus to relax. Pay attention to what you may be feeling and the quality of your thoughts. Are they calm or busy? Do they carry a particular emotion, or a certain memory? Notice any sensations in your body. After a minute or so move the crystal away from you and choose another. Repeat the process and compare the experiences. When you have finished, sit for a few moments with your eyes closed and take slow, deep breaths.

Hold a smoky quartz in your left hand and a clear quartz in your right hand. Sit quietly with your eyes closed, or gaze gently into another crystal. After a few moments change the crystals around to the other hand. What differences do you feel? Once you have found a combination that is comfortable and effective spend a few minutes every day sitting with your crystals.

▼ If you find it difficult to settle down quietly with one crystal use your creative playfulness to make a pattern or mandala with your stones. This form of active contemplation can be just as revealing and relaxing as "doing nothing". If you have space, it can be interesting to make a large mandala of stones on the floor and spend a while sitting in the centre.

▲ Place or hold the crystal at a comfortable distance so that you can easily gaze into the depths of the stone. Don't worry about your thoughts or about "doing it right". Just relax and gaze into the stone. After a few minutes, gently close your eyes. If you feel tension or pressure anywhere take a couple of slow, deep breaths and consciously relax again. Repeat the procedure several times if you wish. Take a little time to return to everyday activity when you decide to finish the meditation exercise.

HAND-HELD CRYSTAL HEALING

Whenever we wish someone well there is a natural flow of healing energy. This can be concentrated and enhanced by the use of quartz crystal in combination with directed thought. Here are a few exercises that use simple imagination or visualization skills to direct healing energy where it is needed. A quartz crystal will direct the flow of energy either towards or away from the body, depending on where the point is facing.

An additional stone can be held in the "absorbing" or "receiving" hand. This will help to direct the healing energy very clearly in your mind and, if you choose an appropriate type of stone, the effects will be enhanced. For example, using a rutilated quartz will focus those energies to do with healing tissues and nerves, while a rose quartz will release emotional stress and calm overactivity. A small crystal sphere is a useful shape for the receiving of energies as it stores and passes on energy in a smooth, even way.

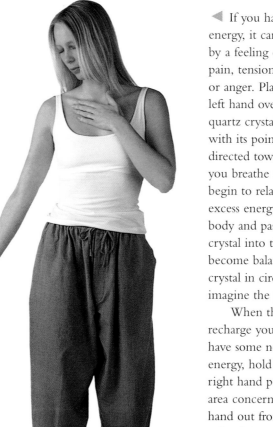

◀ If you have an area of over-energy, it can often be identified by a feeling of congestion, heat, pain, tension, irritation, frustration or anger. Place the palm of your left hand over that area. Hold the quartz crystal in your right hand with its point away from you directed towards the ground. As you breathe deeply and evenly, begin to relax and imagine all excess energy releasing from your body and passing out through the crystal into the earth where it can become balanced. Moving the crystal in circles may help you to imagine the process more clearly.

When there is the need to recharge your vitality or if you have some need for extra healing energy, hold the quartz in your right hand pointing in towards the area concerned. Hold your left hand out from your body with the palm facing upwards. As you breathe deeply and evenly, imagine healing energies from the universe passing from your upturned hand through the crystal and into your body.

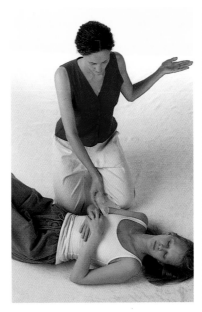

1 You can also apply the hand-held crystal healing method to another person. To clear away unwanted energy, release tensions and help relaxation, hold your "receiving" hand close to them and with the quartz in your "directing" hand allow the excess to drain away into the earth. You may feel that moving the quartz in small circles helps to speed the process. Try out both clockwise and anticlockwise movements to see which feels best.

2 When you finish it is a good idea to recharge the aura with revitalizing energy. So now hold the crystal in the "directing" hand with its point towards the body. Hold your other, "receiving", hand palm upwards and allow universal life energy to flow through the crystal into the newly cleansed area.

▲ Another effective healing method is to sweep a crystal through the subtle bodies. Begin at the feet and slowly move the crystal up the body with increasingly larger circles, always returning to your starting point between the feet. When you have drawn the largest circle reaching to the top of the head, gradually reduce the size of the sweeps and return to your original starting point between the feet, making sure that you focus on that point with a few extra rotations to help "anchor" the energy in a practical way. This is an excellent way to "springclean" someone's aura and remove tensions.

Try these exercises using opposite hands to see how it feels: usually with right-handed people the left hand is more absorbing or "receiving" and the right hand directs the outward flow of energy. If you are left-handed you may find the opposite to be the case.

CRYSTAL PENDULUMS

▶ The correct grip.

▶ A crystal pendulum can be of many types and shapes. Begin with a clear quartz or amethyst.

▼ If the pendulum goes on moving over an imbalance for a long time without seeming to change, put another crystal on that spot and move on. Check later.

Using a crystal pendulum for healing is effective in removing energy imbalances from the body's finer energy systems.

Have a clear intent that the crystal pendulum will only move away from a neutral swing (back and forth), when it comes across an imbalance that can be corrected quickly and safely. The crystal will move in a pattern that allows the imbalance to be cleared and will then return to the neutral swing.

1 Hold the pendulum lightly and firmly between the thumb and forefinger. Allow the wrist to relax and hold arm and body in a comfortable position.

2 Start the pendulum swinging in a line, to and fro. This is a neutral swing.

3 Slowly move up the centre of the body, beginning beneath the feet. Wherever the pendulum moves away from neutral, simply stay at that point until the neutral swing returns.

4 When you get to a point above the head, go back to the feet and begin again, this time holding the pendulum near one side of the body. Repeat for the other side.

CRYSTAL WANDS

Wands are shaped tools which usually have a faceted point at one end opposite a smooth, rounded base. Sometimes natural single crystals are simply given a rounded base, but most are cut from large blocks. The rounded base allows wands to be used directly on the skin without scratching and they can be a lovely adjunct to massage. They are especially useful to release tension from the head, hands and feet. With a light touch, simply move the wand in small circles over the tense areas. Wands can also be used to massage the subtle bodies.

▼ Crystal wands come in all shapes and sizes and can be cut from a wide variety of materials.

1 Begin at the feet with the wand held point outwards and make small anticlockwise circling movements (which help to release unwanted tensions). Slowly work up the body. You will probably be aware of areas that feel different, where the wand feels heavy, sticky or where you feel instinctively inclined to move in a different way. Allow this to happen and then return to the normal movement.

2 When you reach the top of the head, reverse the wand so that the point faces inwards. Move down the body once again in small circles, but this time clockwise. This recharges the body's energy fields. Once again, you may find that certain areas require greater attention.

25

ENVIRONMENTAL PLACEMENTS

Crystals can be useful in many different environments. As well as a decorative focus they can help to reduce the effects of electro-magnetic pollution and emotional stress. Crystals adjust imbalances by absorbing excess energy. A crystal securely positioned in a car, for example, can help to reduce tiredness and improve concentration. For clarity, use clear or citrine quartz.

▲ A large piece of rose quartz or amethyst in the bedroom or living room will help to keep the atmosphere light and positive.

▼ We all get difficult telephone calls from time to time. Keeping a small bowl of tumbled stones or a few favourite crystals by the telephone offers a focus for your attention. It will help to prevent unnecessary depletion of energy, or over-involvement in other people's problems, by helping you to keep a balanced perspective during a tricky conversation.

◀ Computers and VDUs, like all electrical equipment, create quite strong electromagnetic fields around them. Putting a cluster of crystal by the computer screen will help to neutralize the harmful effects. You should notice a reduction in fatigue and irritability. Remember to cleanse the crystal frequently.

CREATING A SACRED SPACE

Creating a sacred space allows you to honour those things that are important in your life. It can be as simple as a photograph and a few flowers or as elaborate as a ritual altar. You may like to arrange meaningful objects to make a temporary special display, and this can be a useful contemplative exercise in itself. You can create a sacred space to record or celebrate a special anniversary or event, or you might like to set aside a permanent quiet space where you can take time to be with your own thoughts and memories.

▼ You can make a mini Zen garden by filling a large, flat bowl with clean sand or fine gravel. Arrange interesting stones and crystals to create a miniature landscape. Use an old comb or fork to draw patterns in the sand.

▲ Adding special crystals brings an extra light and beauty to a sacred space, enlivening and keeping the energies fresh and positive.

▲ A quiet corner of a garden makes an excellent place for quiet reflection, and crystals will enhance a mysterious atmosphere as well as helping to keep the plants healthy.

WEARING CRYSTALS

For thousands of years precious and semi-precious stones have been worn as decoration and for their beneficial properties. Wearing crystals is a useful way to help maintain the body's energy levels, but remember the stone can only help you if its own energy is clean. Place your jewellery on a crystal cluster at night to cleanse it, or, if you have had a difficult time, cleanse them with running water or in incense smoke for a minute. If crystal jewellery isn't cleansed regularly, the stones cannot process unbalanced energies and these may even be reflected back into your auric field, making matters worse.

Crystal jewellery is best used when you need a little extra boost. Wear only one or two stones at a time – more may confuse the energy message to the body. Don't become dependent on your crystals; have a couple of days without any from time to time.

Sometimes a stone needs to be somewhere particular on the body. If you don't have a pocket in the appropriate place, use a small bag or pouch and a safety pin to attach it securely to the inside of your clothing.

◀ A simple way of wearing crystals is as a pendant. The length of the chain used will determine which chakra will be most stimulated and balanced. A stone at the solar plexus will influence how you use your store of energy and what you do with personal power; a stone at the heart will affect your emotional state; placed between the heart and throat a crystal will help you define your space and needs; at the throat, a stone will aid your communication and artistic skills.

Crystal earrings can help to balance throat, neck and head energies.

▶ Wearing gemstone rings will stimulate different meridian channels depending on which fingers they are worn on.

MAKING GEM REMEDIES

Gem remedies are vibrational preparations made by placing a sample of a gemstone in a clear glass bowl of pure spring water and exposing it to direct sunlight. Because of the characteristics of water this process allows the energy pattern of the stone to be imprinted on the water. When it is ready the stone is removed and the charged water is bottled and used for helping the healing processes of the body. A certain amount of care needs to be taken with this procedure as some gemstones are toxic or soluble in water. If you would like to try this yourself, gem water is easy to make.

Take a clean crystal of quartz and place it overnight in a glass of water. The charged water can be drunk in the morning. Or keep a water jug (pitcher) with a couple of crystals in it to energize the contents. Use this water to drink or to water plants. Try gem water made from different members of the quartz family: citrine, amethyst or tiger's eye.

USING CRYSTAL LIGHTBOXES

The qualities and properties of gemstones are recognized and valued for the way they reflect, hold and interact with light. A lightbox is a simple device for directing light through a transparent or translucent crystal.

Putting a crystal on a lightbox can create changes of mood and atmosphere in a room. For instance, a red light or a red crystal will be energizing, yellow will increase relaxation, green will have a calming effect, and violet will create mystery.

▶ You will need a stone with a flat base large enough to cover the aperture. If you want to try a clear quartz, those with some milkiness or cloudiness in the base will work best, diffusing the light evenly throughout the crystal. For different moods use coloured lightbulbs or coloured filters to change the colour of light passing though a clear crystal.

A crystal with internal fractures, rainbows or inclusions, such as moss agate or rutilated quartz, will light up magnificently.

TREATING PLANTS AND ANIMALS

You can use the life-enhancing properties of gemstones and crystals to maintain the health of your pets, or to help them through times when they are unwell. There are three main chakra points on four-legged animals: at the top of the head, halfway along the spine, and at the base of the tail.

Using a pendulum or massage wand to balance your pet's energy bodies can be helpful – you will soon know if your pet thinks otherwise! A simple method to give your pet a boost of energy is to add gem water to the animal's drinking water, or you can put a drop or two on your hands and either stroke it on to the fur or sweep it through the auric field from head to tail several times.

Cats are sensitive to subtle energies and they may not appreciate a lot of crystals placed around them. Dogs tend to be less fussy. Any sick animal will appreciate your efforts to help them but watch for any signs of discomfort. A pet that curls up and goes to sleep close to a crystal in its basket has found the energy comfortable and acceptable. A tiny gemstone can be attached to a dog collar in a small pouch or suspended from the collar by a silver spiral mount.

◀ Crystals in an aquarium show their vivid colours and will energize the surroundings.

▼ Houseplants can also benefit from crystals placed in the top of their pots. Quartz is an excellent stone to use as an overall enhancer of energies. Emerald also has a close affinity with all plants: it needn't be of gem quality – large green beryl crystals are quite easy to acquire. Alternatively you can use aquamarine, a blue variety of the same mineral. Jade is said to amplify the energies of plants and will also help you to attune more closely with them. Turquoise can be used to help plants recover from damage and disease.

CRYSTAL HEALING PLACEMENTS:
THE SEAL OF SOLOMON

The Seal of Solomon is so-called because a six-pointed star, formed from two interlocking triangles, was often used in medieval magical texts ascribed to King Solomon. The symbol represents the interaction of the four elements and the uniting of heaven and earth. The Seal of Solomon can be used whenever there is a need to relax, physically and mentally. It refreshes the body's energies and clears away stress. It can also be used on a specific part of the body that

CLEAR
QUARTZ

needs healing. Depending on where the problem is you may need to have some stones on and some stones off the body. This makes no difference – as long as the stones create the necessary star shape and they remain in the energy field, they will work.

◀ You will need six clear quartz points, which should be placed in a star shape evenly around the body: at head and feet, at shoulder level and knee level. When the points are facing outward there will be a release of any excess energy. When the points face towards the body there will be a charging, energizing effect.

◀ Begin with the points turned outwards for about five minutes, then reverse the stones so that the body is infused with new energy for a minute or two. If you experience any discomfort when the stones are facing in the first direction, try starting with the other placement.

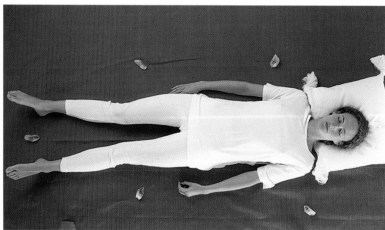

32

◀ To treat a part of the body, place the six quartz stones around the area with the points facing outwards for a while, then replace the crystals in the same positions, with the points facing inwards. It is sometimes appropriate to place another crystal in the centre of the quartz points to act as a focus for the healing energy.

▼ You can intuitively select a stone for the centre of the star shape, or choose one according to its colour code, using green for calming, for example, activating with red, or cooling with blue. Top row, left to right: jasper will gently ground and energize; malachite will reduce pain. Bottom row: turquoise will calm; citrine will relax; sodalite will cool.

JASPER

MALACHITE

TURQUOISE

CITRINE

SODALITE

GROUNDING AND CENTRING

In order to be effective when using crystals for healing, and in order to gain maximum benefit from crystal healing, you need to be centred and grounded. Grounding is a term that means you are solidly anchored in the present, with a certain inner stillness, a feeling of being secure, in control of yourself and alert. When you lack grounding you will feel nervous, unfocused, and unable to concentrate. When dealing with the energy of crystals and the healing process, being grounded enables you to "earth" excess energy and prevents you from becoming overwhelmed or "spaced-out".

Eating and drinking is an effective way to focus your energies into the physical body: a sip of water or tea and a biscuit is often enough. Chocolate will provide enough sugar-shock to bring you down to earth rapidly!

Physical activity, such as stamping your feet, jumping up and down, doing some gardening or a similar task, are all good grounding exercises.

▲ Holding a grounding stone helps to focus your energy, and such stones are a great help in bringing you back to normal, everyday awareness after a healing session. A simple grounding exercise is to sit or stand with your feet firmly placed on the floor and imagine roots growing from your feet deep into the earth. With each breath, allow the roots to spread deeper and wider until you feel firmly anchored and secure.

▼ For a grounding layout, place a smoky quartz crystal point downwards at the base of the throat and a second smoky quartz between the legs or close to the base of the spine, also with its point towards the feet. This is an excellent way to centre and ground your energies in a couple of minutes. In most crystal healing patterns it is a good idea to use a grounding stone close to the base chakra or between the feet or legs. This ensures that the changes created by the crystals are rooted in the physical body and can be integrated in a practical manner.

Being centred means being physically, emotionally and mentally balanced. You are aware of your own boundaries and in control of your energies. It is a state of calm receptivity in which you can more easily be aware of your intuitive thoughts and subtle feelings. Centring can be achieved by any technique that focuses your attention within your body.

1 Sit quietly and spend a minute simply being aware of each breath as it comes and goes.

2 Imagine you are breathing in from your feet and breathing out through your feet into the earth.

3 Become aware of your midline – an imaginary line extending from above the top of your head to below your feet, situated just in front of your spine. Pull your breath into this midline from above and breathe out through the line into the ground. Repeat until you are calm and focused.

4 Strike a bell, gong or tuning fork and simply listen for as long as the sound remains.

5 Focus your attention on the centre of gravity, located within your pelvic girdle behind and below your navel.

6 Slowly and consciously bring your fingertips together and hold them for a minute or two, breathing deeply. As well as centring this also increases mind/body co-ordination.

▲ Bring your fingertips together slowly to focus your attention.

▼ Some gemstones are particularly effective in helping to ground your energies. Most grounding stones are dark or red, like these pictured below. *Top, left to right:* snowflake obsidian, haematite, dark tourmaline, smoky quartz, onyx. *Bottom, left to right:* staurolite, citrine, jasper.

BALANCING AND CALMING CRYSTALS

After a hard day at work it can sometimes take a long time to "wind down" and feel relaxed enough to enjoy your free time. A simple placement of stones can help you to feel calm and refreshed after a couple of minutes.

▼ Clear quartz increases clarity and quietens the mind. Smoky quartz, point downwards, helps release tensions and re-establishes focus in the present. The rose quartz balances the chakra system and the emotions.

ROSE QUARTZ

CLEAR QUARTZ

SMOKY QUARTZ

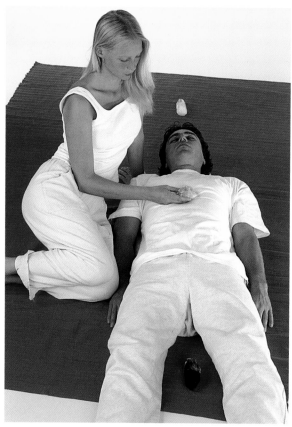

▲ Place a clear quartz crystal, with its point upwards, above the top of the head. Place a smoky quartz crystal, point downwards, close to the base of the spine (between the upper thighs or knees). Put a small rose quartz crystal on the centre of the chest. You should find that four or five minutes is sufficient to feel refreshed.

36

FEELING "OUT OF SORTS"

Sometimes you may feel as though you are jangled and "not quite right". There is no apparent reason for this sense of disorientation but it is as if you have "got out of bed on the wrong side" that morning. This feeling may wear off during the day, but if it continues try the following placement of crystals.

▼ The stones you will need for alleviating a feeling of disorientation.

TURQUOISE

LAPIS LAZULI

CLEAR QUARTZ

SMOKY QUARTZ

▼ Place a clear quartz, point outwards, at the crown of the head. Place a turquoise or lapis lazuli at the centre of the forehead. Finally, place a smoky quartz, point downwards, near the base of the spine.

CALMING THE HEART AND MIND

There are times when you may feel unhappy or tense because of some stressful situation or when you are unable to do or say what you feel you should. This layout of crystals will help to calm an emotional upset and allow you to focus on the practical solutions to the situation.

Signs of stress being released include fast fluttering of the eyelids; deep breaths or sighs; muscle twitches; yawning; tearfulness, crying and sobbing.

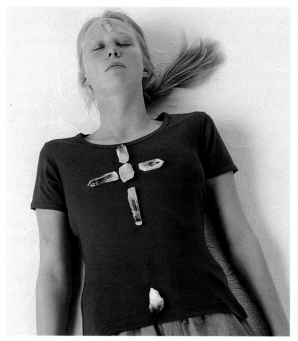

CITRINE

ROSE QUARTZ

CLEAR QUARTZ

AMETHYST

▲ For clearing emotional stress you will need four clear quartz stones together with citrine, rose quartz and an amethyst.

▲ On the centre of the chest, place a small rose quartz surrounded by four clear quartz points. If the points are placed outwards they will help to remove emotional imbalances. If the points are placed inwards they will help to stabilize an over-emotional state. On the lower abdomen, just below the navel, place a citrine quartz with its point directed downwards. This will increase the sense of security and feeling of safety. Place an amethyst on the brow or above the top of the head. This helps to calm the mind. If you feel the release is too strong, remove the stones from the heart area and place a hand over the solar plexus.

ALLEVIATING STRESS AND TRAUMA

A shock, accident or loss may leave you feeling profoundly shaken and insecure. This layout helps you to release stress and gather yourself together again. Look out for the tensing of muscles, mental replays of events and sudden wellings of emotion. Continue regular use of this layout until these signs disappear. This will help to prevent the shock seeping deeply into the system.

▼ For this layout you will need eight small clear quartz crystals, a rose quartz and a tiger's eye.

▼ Place a small rose quartz at the heart centre with four clear quartz points facing outwards, placed diagonally around it. At the sacral centre, below the navel, place a tiger's eye. Surround it with four clear quartz crystals with points inwards, also placed diagonally. The stones at the heart release emotional tension while the stones on the abdomen balance the first, second and third chakras and give stability and grounded energy.

CLEAR
QUARTZ

TIGER'S EYE

ROSE QUARTZ

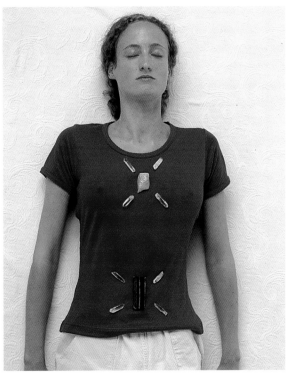

SEVEN COLOUR CHAKRA LAYOUT

One of the simplest ways to help balance the whole chakra system is to place a stone of the appropriate colour on each area. This will give each chakra a boost of its own vibration without altering its energies or the overall harmony of the system. If you lay your collection of stones out so that you can easily see them all you will find your attention goes to the best choice of stone for each chakra. It is a good idea to place a grounding stone, like smoky quartz, between the feet to act as an anchor.

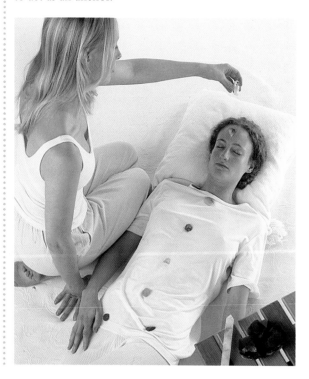

1 Choose a red stone to put near the base of the spine or, alternatively, use two red stones of the same sort and rest one near the top of each leg. This will deal with the base chakra.

2 For the sacral chakra choose an orange coloured stone to put on the lower abdomen.

3 At the solar plexus use a yellow stone, placed between the navel and the ribcage. If there is tension in this area an energy-shifting stone, like a tiger's eye or a small clear quartz point, can be put at the diaphragm to help release.

4 The heart chakra in the centre of the chest can be balanced with a green stone. A pink stone can be added for emotional clearing.

5 For the throat chakra use a light blue stone. Place it at the base of the throat, at the top of the breastbone.

6 An indigo or dark blue stone is normally used to balance the brow chakra in the centre of the forehead. Amethyst or another purple stone can also be used here.

7 The stone for the crown chakra rests just above the top of the head. If you have chosen an amethyst for the brow, use a clear quartz at the crown. If you have used a dark blue stone at the brow you can use a violet stone at the crown.

INTUITIVE HEALING LAYOUTS

You will become more confident at crystal healing when you allow your intuition to guide you to the correct stones and their placement. You will then be able to modify the healing energy to suit different people's needs. "Mistakes" – picking up the "wrong" stone, or putting it in the "wrong" place – are very often an unconscious identification of what is really needed. In order to make appropriate intuitive decisions you need to have a certain understanding of the other person's energy. Begin by using a few simple healing procedures – a balancing layout or a crystal pendulum for example. As you sit watching the other person during the crystal session your attention may go to a particular pattern of stones or an area of the body. This can be an intuitive signal that crystals need to be placed there, or that existing stones need changing in some way. As a practical exercise in developing your intuitive skills try the following healing technique.

1 Lay all your crystals and gemstones out so that you can see them easily, then spend a minute or two either talking together or use a wand or pendulum to give an initial balance to the auric field. With the person's needs in mind go over to your crystals and pick up those that immediately attract your attention. Don't concern yourself about why you might have chosen them.

2 Very quickly, without conscious thought, place the stones where you feel they need to be. Don't concern yourself with the placement – they can be anywhere on or around the body. Keep a check on how the person feels and make adjustments where you feel they are necessary. After about five minutes remove the stones and use a grounding stone to settle the energies back to normal. If you like, recheck how the person's energy feels now using a pendulum or wand.

AMETHYST HEALING LAYOUT

Amethyst quartz is one of the most versatile healing stones. This layout can be used in any situation where physical, emotional or mental healing is required. Most people find they can stay comfortably in this layout for up to half an hour. Try to match the size of crystals as closely as possible to give a balanced feel – odd sized stones may give a rolling sensation.

▲ You will need eight amethysts of roughly equal size, evenly spaced around the body. If you have natural crystals place the terminations so that they are facing inwards towards the body. When you have finished you might like to place a grounding stone, such as smoky quartz or black tourmaline, in the centre of the forehead to help you return to the present. Take time before you resume normal activities.

◀ Amethyst is an ideal healing stone. As it balances and quietens the mind you may become aware of an increased imagination and ability to visualize clearly.

AMETHYST FOR HEADACHES

Amethyst can be very useful in soothing headaches. Headaches tend to occur when there is an imbalance or blockage of energy to the head. This healing pattern helps to free up blocked energies and so reduce the pain.

▶ Place one amethyst point on either side of the base of the neck, just above the collar bones, pointing up towards the top of the head. Place a third stone, also pointing upwards, in the centre of the forehead on the brow chakra. An optional fourth amethyst can be placed, point outwards, at the top of the head.

AMETRINE

▲ Another common cause of headaches is an imbalance between head energy and the solar plexus chakra, usually brought about by stress or unsuitable food. If you suspect this to be the case, or if you have a headache with an upset stomach, use a stone that helps to balance the solar plexus – such as citrine or moonstone. In these instances a piece of ametrine, a natural mix of amethyst and citrine – part golden, part violet – is ideal.

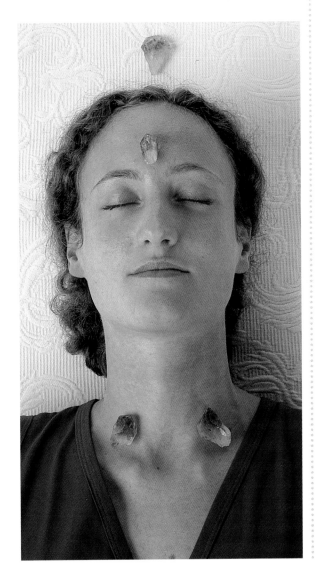

EASING PMT AND MENSTRUAL CRAMPS

Period pains and menstrual cramps are often made worse by physical and emotional tension restricting the body's natural energy flows. Moonstone helps to balance and relax emotional states. It also has beneficial effects on all fluid systems in the body and eases tension in the abdominal area.

▼ A healing pattern of five moonstones amplifies the relaxing and healing potential of the stone. Place one moonstone at the top of your head, one on the front of each shoulder by the armpit and one resting on each hip.

DARK OPALS

MOONSTONES

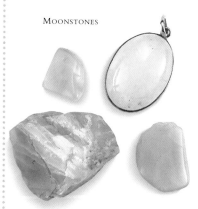

▲ Natural, tumbled and gem polished moonstones. Ancient Indian Ayurvedic texts describe moonstone as the ideal stone for women to wear.

▲ Dark opal has qualities similar to those of moonstone, though it acts more on the first and second chakras where it can often ease menstrual cramps in a very short time. Place a small piece in a hip or trouser pocket. Dark opal is a non-gem variety that can be found in many colours. The most common form is slate grey with an orange translucence.

RELIEVING ACHES AND PAINS

From time to time, everyone suffers from the aches and pains of over-stretched muscles. Sometimes chronic muscle tension can develop from repetitive actions at work, or through maintaining a poor posture at a desk or in the car. Because crystal healing is very relaxing, it will be of general benefit for these sorts of aches and pains. However with really tense, knotted muscles you may need to take a more focused approach.

LODESTONE

▲ Lodestone is the traditional name for magnetic iron ore, used for navigation in ancient times. If you place a small piece near the base of the skull and another at the bottom of the spine, back tensions can be helped and the subtle spinal energies stimulated.

▲ An effective healing pattern to realign the whole body structure uses eight pieces of dark tourmaline (schorl). First, place four tourmalines in a cross shape: above the head, below the feet, and midway down each side of the body. Each of the remaining four stones is positioned slightly clockwise of the others. This pattern may initially focus your attention on the painful areas – but this soon eases away as the body relaxes and readjusts itself.

Release back tension by placing a small, clear quartz on the centre of the forehead. Imagine a beam of bright white light passing deep into your head with each inhalation.

▼ Tourmaline, especially the dark varieties of black and dark green (sometimes known as "schorl" and "verdelite"), is excellent for any structural adjustment. A painful, knotted muscle can be relieved by keeping a piece of tourmaline near to it. Neck, jaw or head tension can be eased by wearing tourmaline earrings, the long thin crystals making elegant pieces of jewellery.

TOURMALINE

RESTORING PEACEFUL SLEEP

Sleepless nights can be caused by a variety of situations. They can often be overcome by simple strategies – but when you are half-asleep and exhausted, motivation is a difficult thing to summon up. This is when the right sort of crystals can be very useful. Different types of sleeplessness will need different gemstones to ease them, and you will need to experiment – a stone that works for one person may keep someone else awake.

CHRYSOPRASE

▲ Chrysoprase, an apple green variety of chalcedony quartz, has been found in most cases to encourage peaceful sleep. A tumbled stone can be put under your pillow, or a larger piece placed on a bedside table.

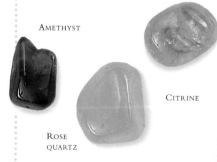

▲ Just hold the appropriate stones or have them nearby. They will help to quieten you so that you can relax and fall asleep.

AMETHYST

CITRINE

ROSE QUARTZ

▲ If tension and worry is the cause of restlessness try amethyst, rose quartz or citrine.

IRON PYRITES

▲ If your sleep pattern is disturbed by something you have eaten, a digestive calmer like ametrine, moonstone or iron pyrites may help.

STAUROLITE

TOURMALINE

SMOKY QUARTZ

▲ Where there is fear, particularly related to bad dreams or nightmares, use a grounding and protecting stone such as tourmaline, staurolite, smoky quartz or tourmaline quartz and place it at the foot of your bed. Labradorite will also help to chase away any unwelcome thoughts and feelings.

RELIEVING PAIN

Pain is the body's way of letting you know that something is wrong and needs attention. Very often pain is caused by an excess of energy of some sort. Using crystals can help reduce pain to manageable levels by releasing blocks within the subtle bodies and stimulating the body's own healing mechanisms. In general, all cool-coloured stones – blue, indigo and violet – will help to calm painful areas and restore the natural flow of energy in a damaged area.

▲ Malachite is a soft mineral of copper that forms in concentric bands of light and dark green. It is good at calming painful areas and drawing out imbalances. It is a good absorber of negativity and needs regular cleansing to maintain its effectiveness.

▲ Turquoise can be used whenever there is a need for calm healing energy. The colour of the stone stimulates the body's immune system and it has a beneficial effect on many areas.

▶ Carnelian, although it is a warm colour, is a useful stone as it is a powerful healer of the etheric body and encourages healing.

CARNELIAN

ROSE QUARTZ

▲ Pink stones, such as rose quartz, calm aggravated areas and also reduce the fears that often accompany injury and pain. Placing pink stones at the solar plexus and sacral chakras will calm the mind and relax the body.

▶ Copper is well-known for its ability to reduce inflammation and swellings of all sorts, and some of the most useful gemstones for controlling pain have high concentrations of copper. Copper itself can be worn as a bracelet or carried in its rough, natural, nugget form to help all energy flow in the body and reduce inflammation.

COPPER

MALACHITE

TURQUOISE

ENERGIZING CRYSTALS

A lack of energy is often felt when the body is in a state of imbalance. Correcting the balance using crystal healing techniques will restore your natural vitality. However, when it is needed you can give yourself an extra energy boost by using those stones that directly stimulate vitality.

▼ Red, orange and yellow stones will promote an increase of energy. Bright, strong colours such as a deep red garnet or a golden amber or topaz will be very stimulating and dynamic. More earthy tones – such as tiger's eye, dark citrine and jasper – will tend to focus on an increase in practical motivation. You may find some stones too energizing in certain situations. For example, golden citrine quartz is a wonderful substitute for the sun's warm energy on a dull winter's day, but you might find it uncomfortable in high summer.

CALCITE

RUTILATED QUARTZ

RUBY

AMBER

JASPER

DARK CITRINE

CARNELIAN

CITRINE

▲ For a quick addition of energy to the whole system hold a clear quartz crystal, point upwards, in each hand and place a large citrine at the solar plexus.

48

AIDING STUDY AND CONCENTRATION

The ability to be effective in learning situations depends upon several factors that can be enhanced by the use of crystals. The mind needs to be clear, focused and alert. Clear quartz brings stillness to the mind, and a grounding stone prevents your mind straying.

▼ Have a favourite quartz crystal near you as you study. Take the stone into a test or examination – it will remind you of what you have learned and will give you extra confidence and clarity.

CITRINE

AMBER

▲ The colour yellow is known to stimulate the logical functions of the mind, so a bright yellow stone like amber, citrine or fluorite will assist memory and recall. Any sort of fluorite is an excellent stone for study as it helps to balance the functioning of the brain hemispheres. This is particularly helpful when you need to do a lot of reading.

KYANITE

SODALITE

SAPPHIRE

▲ Deep blue stones, like kyanite, sodalite and sapphire, will enable clearer communication skills and better understanding of ideas and concepts.

DIRECTORY OF CRYSTALS

Of the many thousands of different minerals on earth, only relatively few are used in crystal healing – mainly those that are abundant and sturdy enough to withstand regular handling. Even so, with all the different varieties and colours available it can be bewildering trying to remember what each stone does and how each can be used. Learning the properties of colour will help you to identify the general functions of a crystal or gemstone.

RED STONES

The colour red stimulates, activates and energizes. It is associated with the first chakra at the base of the spine, which is the centre in the subtle anatomy for action and activity. Ability to use practical skills, movement, motivation, protection, physical survival and the use of life-energy are some of its main functions.

GARNET, in its red varieties, is one of the speediest energizers. It will increase energy wherever it is placed. It will also tend to activate other stones placed nearby.

JASPER, a dark or brick red massive form or quartz, is commonly found on beaches. It is a useful stone to place near the base chakra. It is grounding and gently activating to the functions of the body.

RUBY is a red variety of the very hard mineral, corundum. It works with the energies of the heart centre and the circulation within the subtle anatomies. It is energizing but balancing in its effects.

STAR RUBY

JASPER

JASPER

POLISHED
RUBY CRYSTAL

SECTION OF
RUBY CRYSTAL

GARNET
PEBBLE

GARNET
CRYSTAL

PINK STONES

Pink, a blend of both red and white, has a gentle and subtle way of pushing things towards a resolution. It is related to the actions of the base chakra and the heart chakra, and helps to bring emotions and sensitivity into our daily actions.

ROSE QUARTZ is the best known and favourite of the pink stones. It has a calming and reassuring effect. However, it can also be a powerful releaser of unexpressed emotions where they might be thwarting personal growth.

RHODONITE, when polished, is a salmon pink often flecked with black. This works with the practical aspects of our feelings, and has a greater grounding effect than other pink stones.

KUNZITE is a pale pink and violet stone. Having a striated crystal structure it is an excellent shifter of emotional debris, and also helps self-expression.

RHODONITE

KUNZITE

RHODOCROSITE

ROSE QUARTZ

RHODOCROSITE is a delicate banded stone of pink, yellow and orange. It will help to improve self-image and self-worth, especially when problems in this area are preventing action. It is excellent for balancing the functions of the second and third chakras.

ROSE QUARTZ

ORANGE STONES

Orange is an equal mix of red and yellow, and this combines energizing and focusing qualities. It is associated with the second chakra, which deals with the flow or lack of flow within the body. Creativity and artistic skills are an expression of this flow, while shock, trauma and blocks indicate the lack of flow.

CARNELIAN is the most popular orange stone, characterized by a sense of warmth and a gently energizing effect. It is commonly found on beaches. It will nearly always be of benefit in healing.

ORANGE CALCITE is smooth and lustrous. It is ideal for the delicate encouragement of potential, and because of its softness and watery feel, is good at melting away problems.

DARK CITRINE, orange and browny-orange, is a balanced stimulator that will bring out practical creative skills. It can be used as a gentle grounding and supporting stone.

TOPAZ, with its elongated crystal form and parallel striations running its length, is an excellent clearing stone that can be used to direct energy around the body.

COPPER, which can be found as natural nuggets and crystallized forms, is ideal for use when a lack of flow creates stagnation and clumsiness. It has a beneficial effect on many physical and subtle systems.

TOPAZ

NATIVE
COPPER

ORANGE
CALCITE

CARNELIAN

CARNELIAN

DARK CITRINE

YELLOW STONES

Yellow relates to the solar plexus chakra that regulates the functioning of the nervous system, digestive and immune systems and the ability to discriminate and identify things. Stress, fear, happiness and contentment are all linked to this colour.

AMBER, a fossil tree resin, varies in colour from a lemon yellow to a rich orange brown, including a deep red and green. It has a beneficial effect on the nervous system and self-healing processes.

RUTILATED QUARTZ is a clear or smoky crystal containing fine threads of golden or orange rutile crystals. It is excellent for moving healing energy from place to place, and works well with broken or damaged tissues.

TIGER'S EYE is a variety of quartz with a velvety sheen that looks like a sweet. The packed fibres and the bands of browns, golds and reds speed up energy flow and anchor subtle changes into the physical body.

CITRINE QUARTZ is a popular yellow stone. When it is a bright, clear yellow it will help to keep the mind clear and focused.

IRON PYRITES, known as "fool's gold", helps to cleanse and strengthen. It calms the digestive system.

TIGER'S EYE

CITRINE

AMBER

IRON PYRITES CRYSTAL

RUTILATED QUARTZ

TIGER'S EYE

GREEN STONES

Green is found in the middle of the spectrum and it is associated with the heart chakra, located at the midpoint of that system. Emotions and relationships are balanced here and the qualities needed for growth and personal space are encouraged.

GREEN AVENTURINE is an excellent heart balancer. It is gently expansive, allowing for an easy expression of feelings.

MALACHITE will dig out deep feelings, hurts and resentments and will break unwanted ties and patterns of behaviour.

BLOODSTONE is a green quartz with flecks of red jasper, giving it an active balance of energy and calm. It stimulates emotional growth and is of benefit to the heart and circulation.

AMAZONITE calms and balances the emotions and helps throat and lung problems.

MOSS AGATE is ideal for supporting the lungs and easing breathing difficulties, as well as feelings of being emotionally stifled. It brings in the energy of the natural world.

PERIDOT is a vivid light green stone associated with volcanic activity. It is one of the best cleansers of the subtle bodies and will help to motivate growth and necessary change.

EMERALD, the green variety of the mineral beryl, is a help to finding personal direction in activity. It brings clarity and calm to the heart and emotions.

LIGHT BLUE STONES

The throat chakra, associated with communication, works with this colour. Communication using sight, voice, colour, taste, smell – all the senses – is involved at this centre, as are inner forms of communication: the way you talk to yourself, your thoughts and the ability to express yourself all come under the vibration of light blue.

AQUAMARINE, a blue variety of beryl, stimulates the healing properties of the body. It improves confidence and the ability to stand your ground, and helps to release the flow of communication.

TURQUOISE has been used for centuries as a supportive and protective stone. It strengthens all the subtle bodies and the fine communication systems of the body, such as the meridians.

BLUE LACE AGATE is a beautiful, banded variety of quartz that gently cools and calms. It can be used for lightening thought and works well with rose quartz.

CELESTITE is a soft stone that forms clear, delicate blue crystals. Very inspiring and "dreamy" in its qualities, it is ideal for lifting heavy moods and helps with difficulties in expressing spiritual thoughts and needs. It is also helpful for throat problems.

CELESTITE
CRYSTAL

AQUAMARINE
CRYSTAL

TURQUOISE

TURQUOISE

AQUAMARINE

ROUGH
BLUE LACE AGATE

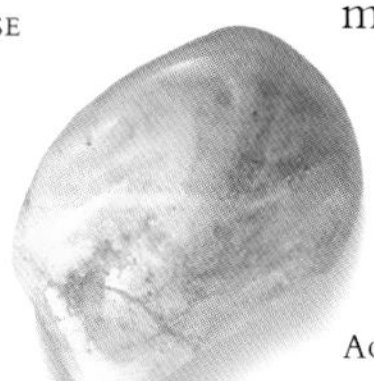

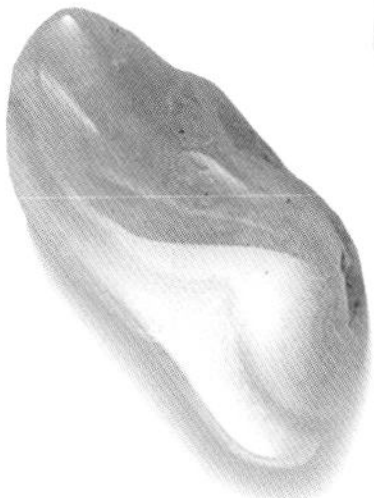

TUMBLED
BLUE LACE AGATE

56

INDIGO STONES

The brow chakra, the "third eye", is linked to the midnight blue of indigo. Perception, understanding and intuition are qualities of this chakra, together with a deep sense of peace and connection.

LAPIS LAZULI is a rock of different minerals that has a large proportion of deep blue lazurite as well as often being flecked with iron pyrites. It has a powerful effect, stimulating the rapid release of stresses to enable a greater peace to be experienced. Lapis also stimulates the higher faculties of the mind and understanding.

SODALITE can look very similar to lapis lazuli, though it is usually of a less vivid blue and has cloudy veils of white running through it. It calms the mind and allows new information to be received.

KYANITE forms translucent thin blades of crystal that often look like fans. A wonderful mover of energy that is blocked or inflamed, it is calming and clearing and is a rapid restorer of equilibrium to all areas.

AZURITE is most commonly seen as small round nodules but can also forms shiny crystals. It will free up difficult and long-standing blocks in communication and will reveal those structures that are stopping us from using our full potential. It stimulates memory and recall.

SAPPHIRE can be expensive when it possesses the correct depth of colour, otherwise you can find good-sized crystals at a reasonable cost. It relaxes and improves the mind. It balances all aspects of the self by releasing tension and promoting peace of mind.

SODALITE

AZURITE

SAPPHIRE

LAPIS LAZULI

KYANITE

SAPPHIRE CRYSTAL

57

VIOLET STONES

Violet and purple are linked to the crown chakra located above the top of the head. Inspiration, imagination, empathy and the sense of service to others are the energies of this centre. Violet and purple stones help to re-balance extremes within the systems of the body, so they can be of use when you are not sure of the nature of a problem.

AMETHYST is perhaps the most useful all-purpose healing crystal. It is universally applicable in its uses and benefits. Amethyst is a good stone to use with meditation as it quietens the mind and allows finer perceptions to become clear.

FLUORITE comes in a wide variety of colours, though violet is one of the commonest. It can be used to great effect with the upper chakras where it enables subtle energies to integrate better with normal consciousness, increasing the practical use of ideas and inspirations. Fluorite also helps with co-ordination, both physical and mental.

SUGILITE is a stone with various shades of purple. It can be useful in group situations where it helps to resolve personal difficulties and brings greater group coherence. This stone is also indicated for those who are uncomfortable with their circumstances or who feel as though they don't "fit in".

IOLITE is also called water sapphire, but is no relation. It has a subtle violet translucence that increases the imagination and all aspects of intuitive creativity.

FLUORITE

AMETHYST

FLUORITE

IOLITE

SUGILITE

WHITE STONES

White or clear stones are often used at the crown chakra where they reflect the qualities of universality and clarity of that centre. White light contains within it all other colours, so it symbolizes the potential to reflect all energies. White stones also reflect the energies around them. White is related to the concepts of clarity, cleansing and purification.

CLEAR QUARTZ strengthens and brings coherent energy, as does milky quartz, which has a gentler effect. All the subtle systems of the body are enhanced and clarified. A state of harmony is brought about.

HERKIMER DIAMOND is a clear, bright variety of quartz excellent for all detoxification processes and for cleansing imbalances from the subtle bodies. It will amplify the qualities of the stones placed near to it. Clarity of mind and vivid recall of dream states are commonly induced.

ICELAND SPA is a variety of clear calcite that helps us to relate to the world in a balanced and productive way, with clarity.

MOONSTONE (see p44) is white, milky, creamy or pearly in colour. It has a characteristic soft luminescence from which it gets its name. It is an excellent stone for clearing tensions gently from the emotions and from the abdomen, where it can help the digestive system. Moonstone will work well wherever there is imbalance in the fluid systems of the body.

SELENITE WAND

CLEAR QUARTZ

ICELAND SPA
(OPTICAL CALCITE)

HERKIMER
DIAMOND

SELENITE, also named for its soft moonlight quality, is a type of gypsum. Do not place this stone in damp or wet – the thin slices of crystal will slide apart and disintegrate. Selenite is a good stone for removing emotional turmoil or confusion. It clarifies awareness and helps to reach new states of consciousness.

BLACK STONES

While white stones reflect and clarify light, black stones absorb light. White will reflect the visible, black will show you the hidden potential of any situation. Black is solidifying and manifesting. It holds all energies quietly within itself and so requires patience to explore fully. Black stones are usually grounding, acting as energy anchors to help you return to a normal functioning state. Many will also reveal hidden aspects so that they can be dealt with – in this respect black stones have a purifying role.

SMOKY QUARTZ is a gentle grounding stone. It is protective and is able to dissolve negative states. It will reach to deep levels of the self to cleanse and balance, and so can be a useful meditation stone. Smoky quartz has all the qualities of clear quartz expressed in a steadier, gentler manner.

OBSIDIAN is volcanic glass. It can be pure black or have flecks of white (snowflake obsidian), patches of red (mahogany obsidian) or a smoky translucence (Apache tears). Obsidian is excellent at bringing imbalance to the surface so that other stones can clear it away. It can also be used to find the hidden factors around situations so that the right action can be taken.

TOURMALINE comes in all colours but the black variety is called "schorl". It is a good protective stone, grounds energies with great speed, and will help to realign physical problems to do with the skeleton and muscles. As a long thin crystal with parallel striations, schorl is a very good energy shifter.

HAEMATITE is an iron ore that can be rust red but is more often a silvery grey with a metallic sheen. It will help the assimilation of iron within the body and has a supportive, grounding and centring effect. It is quietening and calming to the mind.

SNOWFLAKE OBSIDIAN

HAEMATITE

BLACK TOURMALINE

SMOKY QUARTZ

OBSIDIAN

MULTICOLOURED STONES

There are many gemstones and minerals in which a mix of colours occurs naturally. You can determine their actions from the colour combinations that they display. In general, stones that display a full spectrum of colour, or that contain rainbow fractures, will be able to reflect a wide range of states and qualities and can therefore be used for a variety of reasons. Stones with a combination of two colours have specific functions determined by those colours.

OPAL is perhaps the best known of the multicoloured stones. With a high water content which refracts light in a multitude of ways, opal works with the emotional balance. Depending on the play of colour, the opal will naturally harmonize with different chakras.

AZURITE-MALACHITE is a mix of these two related minerals. It allows the deepest imbalances to surface and then be removed. It will also help you to express your needs in a clear, direct way.

LABRADORITE appears a dull waxy grey until it catches the light when beautiful iridescent sheets of peacock blues, yellows and oranges appear. Labradorite will deflect any unwanted energies from the aura.

HAWK'S EYE is a blue variety of tiger's eye with gold, green and orange between deep blue strands. It is ideal for the throat, brow and crown chakras, where its rapid energy enhances the flow of information into the body.

AMETRINE is a quartz which shares the colours and qualities of amethyst and citrine, being part violet and part golden. It balances the mind, augmenting the imagination and the rational mind.

LABRADORITE

HAWK'S EYE

AMETRINE

TOURMALINE

AZURITE-MALACHITE

WATERMELON TOURMALINE

OPAL

BIRTHSTONES

When you go into a jeweller's or a crystal shop it is likely that you will see stones assigned to each of the astrological signs of the zodiac. The attribution of birthstones has a long tradition and is well worth examining. Most of the lists today, however, have been compiled by the jewellery trade to ensure a good sale of different gemstones throughout the year.

▼ Most stones are associated with astrological signs and planets.

AYURVEDIC SYSTEM

SUN	Ruby, garnet, star ruby, red spinel, red zircon, rose quartz.
MOON	Pearl, moonstone, quartz.
MERCURY	Emerald, aquamarine, peridot, green zircon.
MARS	Coral, carnelian, red jasper.
VENUS	Diamond, white sapphire, white zircon.
JUPITER	Yellow sapphire, yellow pearl, topaz, citrine.
SATURN	Blue sapphire, amethyst, lapis lazuli.

THE AYURVEDIC SYSTEM
The oldest known system of correspondence between the planets and gemstones comes from the Indian system of Ayurveda. Here, the positive and negative influence of the planets is assessed and, where necessary, gemstones are suggested to enhance health and success. Large, high quality gemstones are cut and set in the appropriate metals according to carefully laid down procedures and ritual. The individual's circumstances are considered to ensure maximum benefit.

◀ The chart shows the Ayurvedic correspondences between planets and gemstones.

TRADITIONAL BIRTHSTONES

The Western system of attributing gemstones to planets and zodiac signs also has a long tradition, beginning in classical Greek and Roman times. Later it was influenced by the Arabs, who knew of the Indian system.

Medieval thought was dominated by the concept of macrocosm and microcosm, where everything reflected the order within the universe. All animals, plants, colours, gemstones and times of day were thought to fall under the "rulership" of a planet.

Our present-day idea of birthstone lists derives from these traditional systems but they should be taken as only a rough guide at best. As individuals with unique patterns of energy and changing needs, it is more appropriate for us to use those crystals that appeal to us, rather than feel we should wear a designated birthstone. This list is a compilation of the stones most frequently associated with each astrological sign.

AQUARIUS	*(20 Jan – 18 Feb)* Garnet, turquoise, amethyst, onyx, ruby, diamond, jade, ulexite, sapphire.
PISCES	*(19 Feb – 20 Mar)* Amethyst, turquoise, pearl, rose quartz, calcite, aquamarine, bloodstone.
ARIES	*(21 Mar – 20 Apr)* Bloodstone, carnelian, jasper, diamond, aquamarine, emerald, ruby, coral, haematite.
TAURUS	*(21 Apr – 20 May)* Rose quartz, emerald, diamond, tourmaline, tiger's eye, topaz, lapis lazuli.
GEMINI	*(21 May – 20 Jun)* Citrine, tiger's eye, pearl, moonstone, agate, emerald, aquamarine, calcite.
CANCER	*(21 Jun – 20 Jul)* Emerald, chrysoprase, pearl, ruby, moonstone, amber.
LEO	*(21 Jul – 21 Aug)* Clear quartz, onyx, turquoise, ruby, topaz, sunstone, emerald, cat's eye.
VIRGO	*(22 Aug – 22 Sept)* Carnelian, moonstone, sapphire, opal, peridot, sodalite, rutile quartz.
LIBRA	*(23 Sept – 22 Oct)* Peridot, topaz, opal, lapis lazuli, aventurine, emerald, jade.
SCORPIO	*(23 Oct – 22 Nov)* Aquamarine, dark opal, turquoise, obsidian, smoky quartz, herkimer diamond.
SAGITTARIUS	*(23 Nov – 20 Dec)* Topaz, turquoise, garnet, amethyst, malachite, flint, blue lace agate.
CAPRICORN	*(21 Dec – 19 Jan)* Ruby, turquoise, jet, black onyx, clear quartz, black tourmaline.

INDEX